CARILLON

Historical Park

CARILLON

Historical Park

A PLACE IN HISTORY

ORANGE *frazer* PRESS
Wilmington, Ohio

ISBN 978-1939710-352
Copyright©2016 Dayton History

No part of this publication may be reproduced in any material form (including
photocopying or storing in any medium by electronic means and whether or
not transiently or incidentally to some other use of this publication) without
the written permission of the copyright holder except in accordance with the
provisions of the Copyright, Designs and Patents Act 1988.

Published for Dayton History by:
Orange Frazer Press
P.O. Box 214
Wilmington, OH 45177
Telephone: 937.382.3196 for price and shipping information.
Website: www.orangefrazer.com
Book and cover design: Alyson Rua and Orange Frazer Press

Library of Congress Control Number: 2015947316

Printed in China.

The publication of this booklet was made possible through the generosity of:
David and Colleen Brethen, Robert and Carolyn Brethen,
Teresa Huber, John and Karen Marshall, and
Grismer Tire & Auto Service

Photos courtesy of:
Lauryn Bayliff, 26, 37, 46, 60
Carillon Park Archive, 7, 28, 49
Brady Kress, 6, 9, 11, 12–13, 14, 17, 18, 22, 25,
28, 29, 33, 35, 36, 40, 50, 58, 59, 60, 61
Mainsail Productions, 2
Dan Patterson, 42–43, 44–45
Perfect Perspectives, 62
Skip Peterson, 15, 16, 21, 23, 27, 30–31, 34,
36, 38–39, 40, 41, 47, 53, 54, 57
Haylie Schlater, 5, 7, 8, 10, 18, 20, 22, 24, 25,
27, 28, 32, 48, 51, 52, 53, 54, 55, 56, 58, 59
U! Creative, 18, 19

Introduction

Welcome. Carillon Historical Park is a private not-for-profit outdoor history museum—a collection of buildings and unique artifacts exhibited to illustrate remarkable stories and achievements. It is an institution that's dedicated to sharing the stories of local individuals who changed the world with their genius, initiative, and enthusiasm.

Few regions throughout history have accomplished more in such a relatively short time than Dayton, Ohio. It has more patents issued per capita than any other city; more international leaders in aviation, manufacturing, and business; more trailblazers in defense materials, space exploration, flood prevention, and computing. The collected buildings, artifacts, and photographs cannot communicate separately the full importance of Dayton's gifts to the world. Nonetheless Carillon Park always strives to provide today's guests with an experience that is enjoyable, educational, and relevant to their lives today.

Please enjoy strolling through Carillon Park and learning about our region's team of problem solvers, who in the process of realizing their dreams, pushed the boundaries of science and improved the quality of life for people around the world.

Brady Kress,
Dayton History President & CEO

Top: Deeds Carillon stands as one of Dayton's most recognizable symbols, playing concerts year-round both manually and electronically, and tolling daily on the quarter hour.

Left: Listed on the National Register of Historic Places, the Deeds Carillon is Ohio's largest at 151 feet and has 57 bells. Its Art Deco design is cut from Indiana limestone and affixed to a steel frame.

Right: Edith Walton Deeds and Col. Edward A. Deeds began construction of Deeds Carillon in 1940. Col. Deeds served as Board Chairman of the National Cash Register Co. and President of the Miami Conservancy District.

Inset: The famed Olmsted Brothers were contracted to design Carillon Park's landscape including the hewn stone entry gates.

Arranged along Carillon Park's "Town Greene," brick, log, stone, and timber frame structures from the 19th century illustrate the region's wide variety of available construction materials.

Left: Dayton was known as the City of a Thousand Factories. Hundreds of artifacts relating to industry and invention are displayed in the Heritage Center of Dayton Manufacturing and Entrepreneurship.

National Cash Register Company called Dayton, Ohio, home for 125 years. Inventions and products are displayed among architectural remnants of the NCR factory complex.

J. & J. RITTY.
Cash Register and Indicator.

No. 221,360.   **Patented Nov. 4, 1879.**

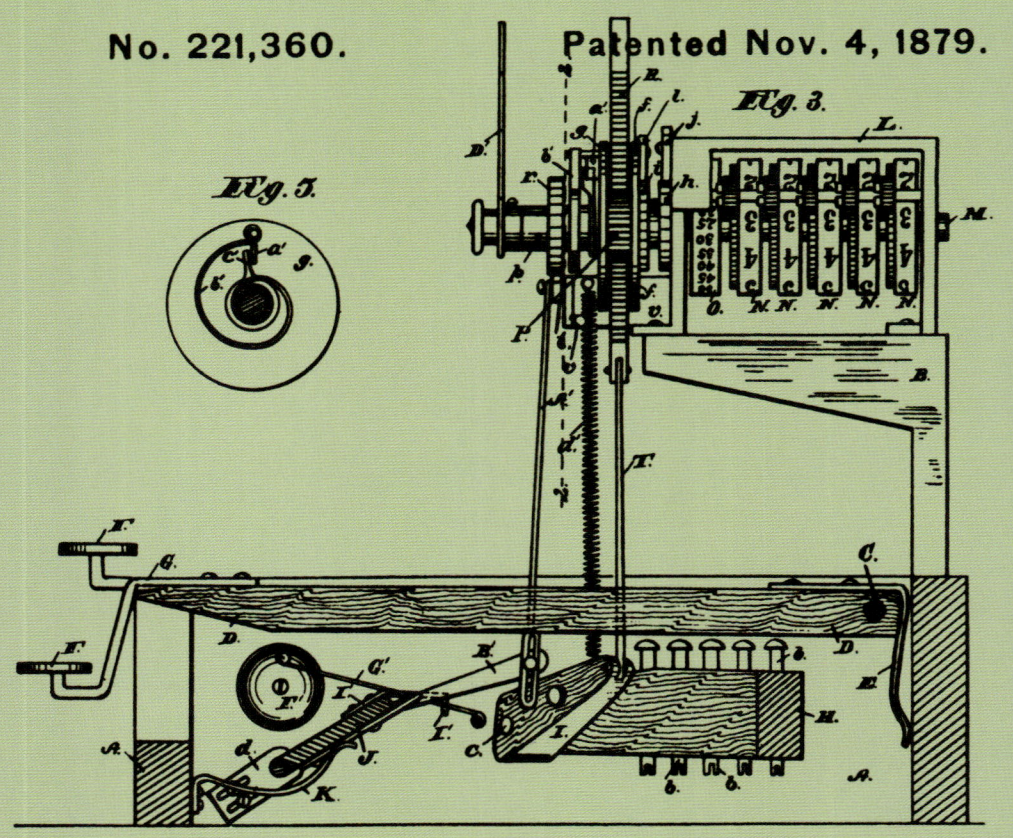

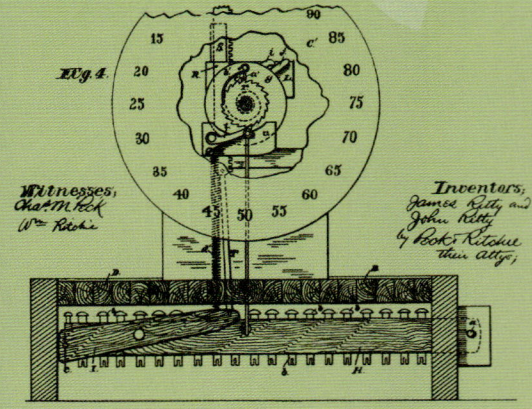

Tired of losing profits to corrupt employees, Daytonians James and John Ritty invented and patented the cash register in 1879.

John and Frank Patterson so believed in the future of the Ritty invention that in 1884 they bought controlling interest in The National Manufacturing Company and changed the name to National Cash Register Company.

Early NCR machines were elaborately carved and inlaid pieces of cabinetry intended to be placed in full view of customers as a symbol of a trustworthy merchant.

John Patterson devised detailed standards and procedures for selling NCR machines, earning him the reputation as the Father of American Salesmanship.

Sold in varying climates around the world, NCR soon replaced their wooden cabinets with ones cast in brass that were resistant to fluctuations in temperature and humidity.

Over 250 NCR machines are on display throughout Carillon Park. NCR's intricately designed brass, nickel, and wood registers controlled the world's business machine market leading into World War I.

Dayton's numerous manufacturers of wood, steel, and friction-propelled toys provided much inspiration in helping to establish Dayton as the birthplace of the soapbox derby.

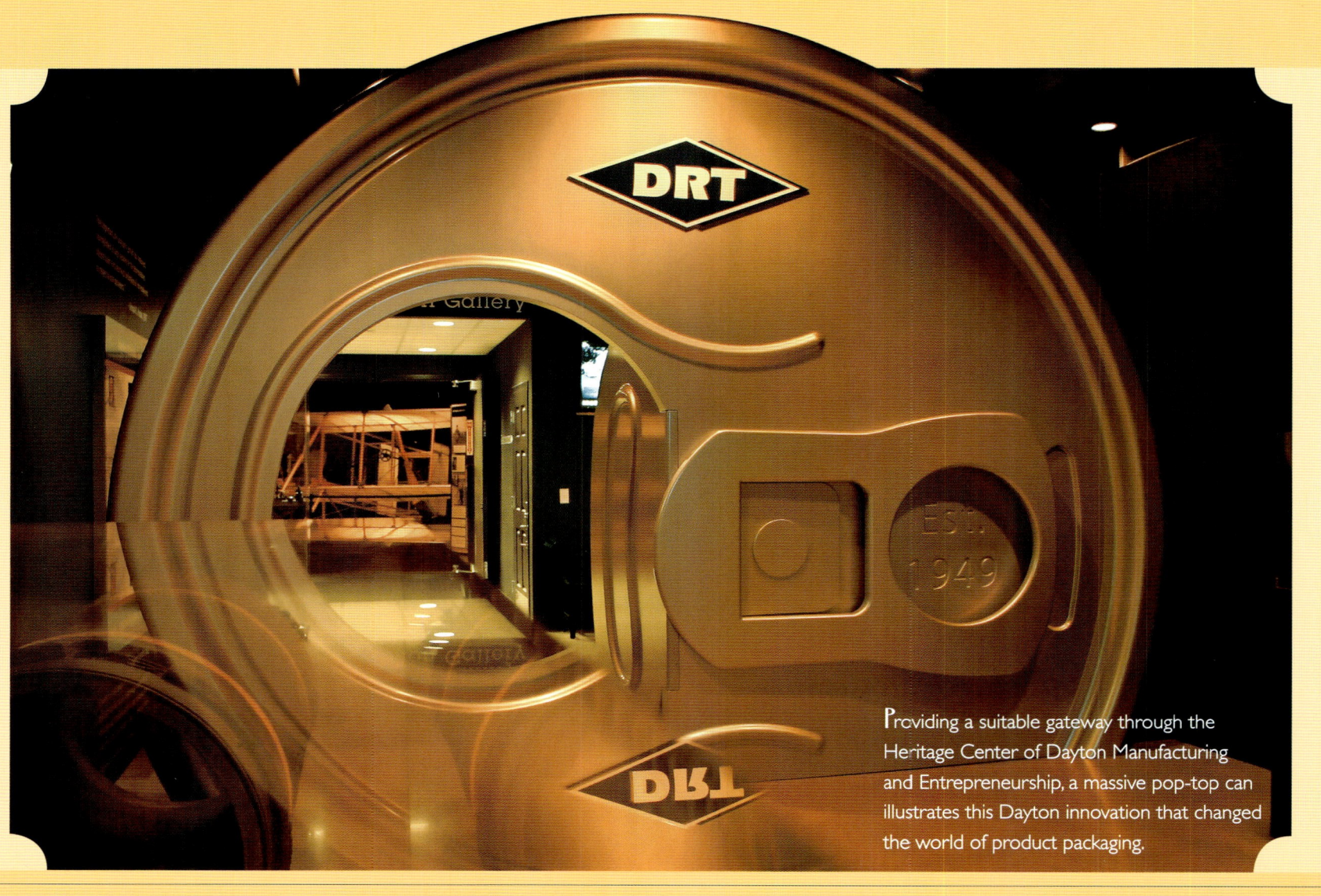

Providing a suitable gateway through the Heritage Center of Dayton Manufacturing and Entrepreneurship, a massive pop-top can illustrates this Dayton innovation that changed the world of product packaging.

Carillon Park's Carousel of Dayton Innovation provides a dynamic illustration of artifacts and stories told throughout Carillon Park. Each hand-carved, custom-painted figure brings to life a brilliant symbol of Dayton's past.

Nestled among the sycamore and cottonwood trees sits the only remaining structure from the Watervliet Shaker community. Inside, guests view examples of the furniture, packaged seeds, and various handicrafts for which the Shakers are known.

Throughout the year, Carillon Park's Locust Grove School No. 12 welcomes thousands of students. Inside the one room slates, oil lamps, and a stern lesson await.

Newcom Tavern stands as Dayton's oldest surviving structure. Built in 1796 of hewn steeple jointed logs, Newcom is presented with its early 19th century sash-sawn, face-nailed, oak siding.

Traditional woodworking demonstrations helped to produce replacement materials for Newcom Tavern. Hand-hewing logs into timber takes a strong back and a good eye.

Limestone was plentiful south of Dayton as showcased in the 1815 William Morris farmhouse. The thick stone walls helped to keep the residents cool in the summer and warm through the Ohio winters.

Good food still flows from the 200-year-old Morris hearth. From the cellar, field, or market, seasonality played a larger role than choice in determining what would come to the table.

Dayton's 19th century residents followed the popular building styles of the day, including this small but classic Greek Revival home.

Flintlock musket loading and firing demonstrations are the highlight of early settlement workshops.

Impressive in size and scope, this 210-ton Corliss steam engine produced electricity to power the NCR factory from 1902 through 1948.

The classic linotype machine is among a full shop of working letterpress printing equipment common in the 1930s.

Mind your ps and qs. Reading upside down and backwards was a practiced trait of the skilled composer, preparing individual pieces of type for the press.

The Sun Oil Company of 1924 was the first to standardize the shape and colors of all its stations. This example stood near Brown and Warren Streets in Dayton.

Left: The Buckeye Manufacturing Company built this 1909 Lambert on display. John William Lambert is credited with building America's first automobile in 1891 near Ohio City, Ohio.

Below: One hundred years of DELCO and General Motors engineering and production is captured near the original Deeds Barn, birthplace of the automobile self-starter.

The beauty of this classic steam powered water pumper is preserved in The Great 1913 Flood exhibit.

A stroll through Carillon Park brings guests up close to architectural remnants such as this 15,000 pound clock which once towered over downtown Dayton on the Callahan Building.

Wheelwise
Not an Ordinary Exhibit

Dayton is home to the Huffy Bicycle Company. Originally a sewing machine company, by 1977 Huffy Corporation was the world's largest producer of bicycles.

COLUMBIA BRIDGE WORKS DAYTON·O

Built in 1881 at Columbia Bridge Works, this bridge spanned Tom's Run on Gratis Road near Farmersville, Ohio. The company's founder, David Morrison, served as Dayton's first city engineer.

Wright Brothers

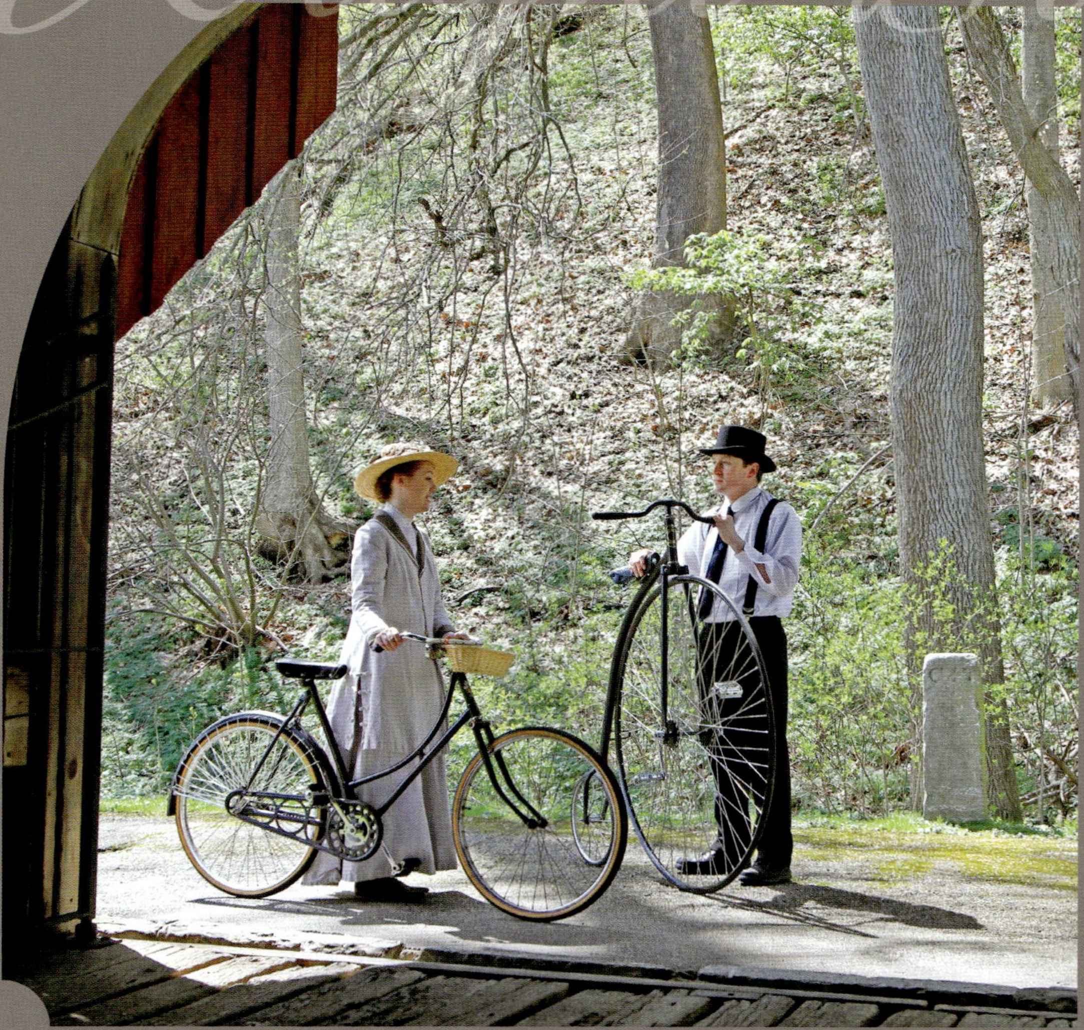

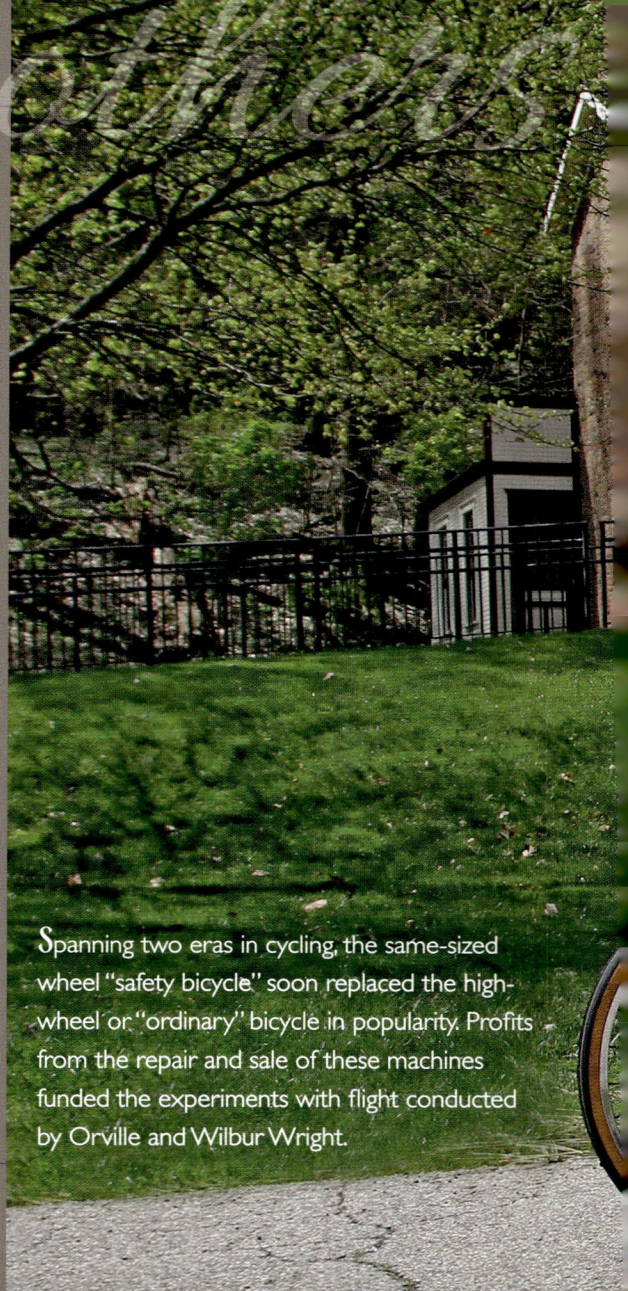

Spanning two eras in cycling, the same-sized wheel "safety bicycle" soon replaced the high-wheel or "ordinary" bicycle in popularity. Profits from the repair and sale of these machines funded the experiments with flight conducted by Orville and Wilbur Wright.

The Wright brothers found it necessary to test their own wing profiles in a homemade wind tunnel in the back of their cycle shop after proving the written research on the subject insufficient.

The world's largest collection of Wright brother artifacts are found at Carillon Park, including the Wrights' camera, drafting table, and sewing machine, on which they prepared the wing coverings.

The 1905 Wright Flyer III is the only aircraft designated a National Historic Landmark. Orville Wright considered it to be the world's first practical airplane.

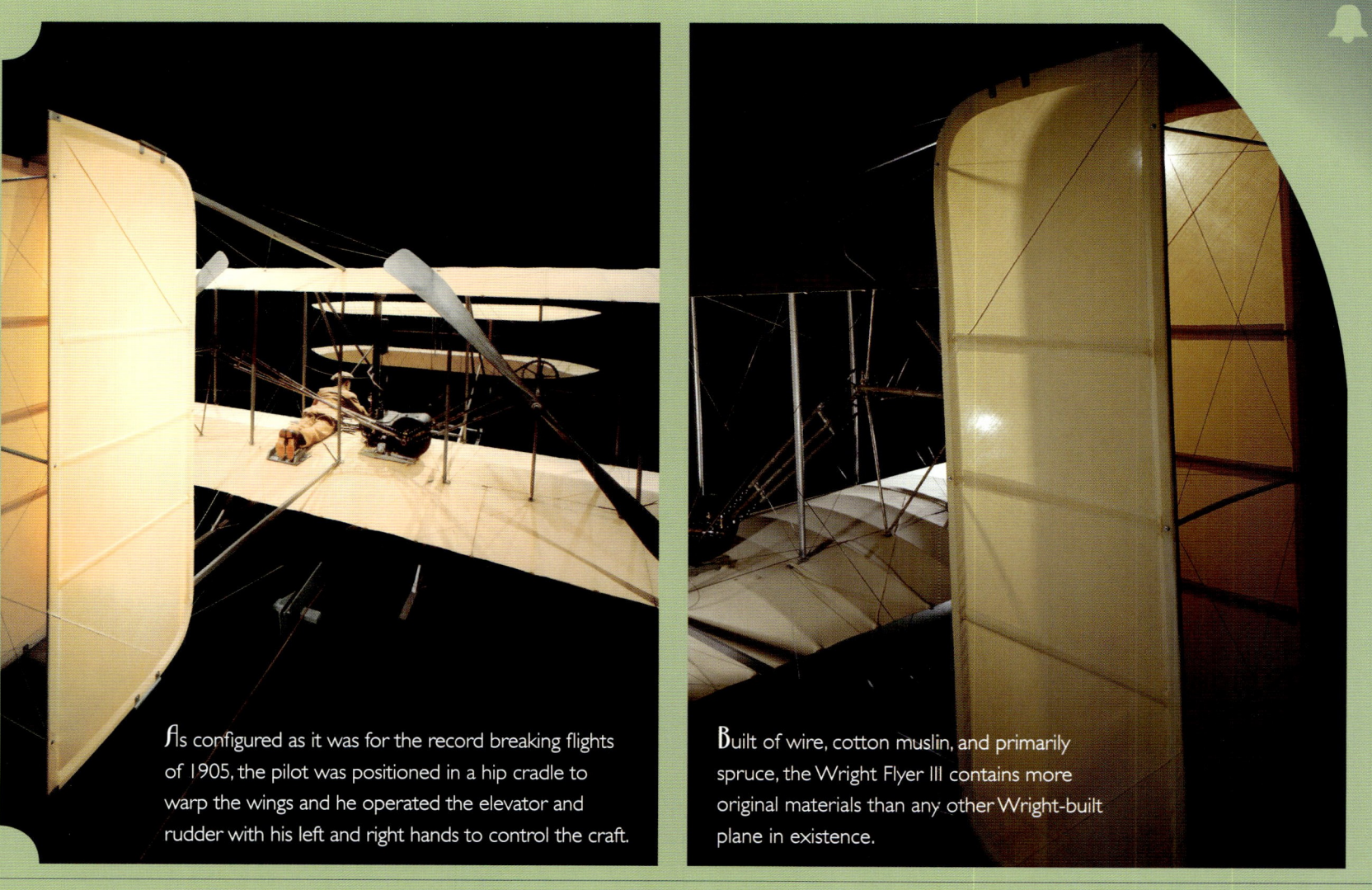

As configured as it was for the record breaking flights of 1905, the pilot was positioned in a hip cradle to warp the wings and he operated the elevator and rudder with his left and right hands to control the craft.

Built of wire, cotton muslin, and primarily spruce, the Wright Flyer III contains more original materials than any other Wright-built plane in existence.

Although the Wrights attempted to do their flight experiments in privacy, they painted the wooden components of their craft gray, so that onlookers would mistake it for metal.

Right down to the smallest fastener, the Wrights used the tools and materials they had been accustomed to using for their bicycle manufacturing.

Dayton's most recognized brothers worked together to design, build, and fly the world's first piloted, heavier-than-air, powered, controllable flying machine.

Orville Wright's final project was to assist his friend Edward Deeds in the design of Wright Hall and the restoration of the 1905 Wright Flyer III at Carillon Park.

Carillon Park's archaeology adventure zone provides a hands-on opportunity to learn how artifacts from the property's former hospital and pre-historic earthwork can be uncovered, identified, and cataloged.

Southwest Ohio's landscape was shaped by the most recent ice age. Massive retreating glaciers left the moraine on which some of Carillon Park is formed.

Culp's baked goods, produce, lunch counters, and cafeteria were a constant presence in downtown Dayton for over 50 years. A delicious meal and a moment to relax can still be enjoyed at Culp's Café at Carillon Park.

Reminiscent of the dozens of commercial breweries that dotted southwest Ohio in the 19th century, the Carillon Brewing Co. exhibits the production of ales using period tools and brewing techniques. Daily demonstrations by costumed interpreters fill the air with aromas of wood smoke, ground barley, and hops.

A massive brick hearth is center stage for all who visit America's only working production brewery in a museum. Surrounding the boil furnace are oak barrel fermenters. It's in these vessels that yeast turns sweet wort into beer.

Above: Costumed interpreters use white oak dippers to transfer hot water for lautering and sparging, and deliver boiled wort through a filtering hopper leading into the cooling ship for eventual fermentation.

The entire historic brewing process takes place in full view of Carillon Park's guests. Once fresh water is drawn to the hot water kettle, the remaining process is stepped downward using gravity to feed the transformation of water into wort, and wort into beer.

Left: Carillon Park's brewery is also a full service restaurant. Hearty 19th century inspired meals are served among the sash-sawn timbers, wood fired brick, hand-built tables, and coal-gas lamps.

Inset: Once guests watch the historic brewing process, uniquely found at Carillon Park, they may taste and purchase the finished product to take home.

CARILLON
BREWING CO.
Premium ales Dayton, O. Hearty Fare
1850

CARILLON
BREWING C?
Premium Ales & Hearty Fare
The DAYTON O. 1850

Historic foodways are demonstrated in numerous locations throughout Carillon Park. The baking of breads in the Hetzel House and the Carillon Brewing Co. bake ovens is a common sight.

Right: Carillon Park's brewery specializes in the production of spent-grain breads. These barley grains have gone through the brewing process, releasing some of their starches for the beer. The grain is used a final time to supplement hearty loaves of bread.

Seasonal feasts are part of the Carillon landscape. Intimate gatherings feature hearth-cooked meals with costumed interpreters and are shared in the candlelit rooms of Newcom Tavern.

Over 75 years of celebrations have occurred in the shadow of Deeds Carillon. Memorial Day fireworks, Christmas concerts, Easter sunrise services, and many other regional events have relied on Ohio's largest carillon to commemorate special moments.

Deeds Carillon stands as a testament to Dayton, Ohio's resilience. Its location along the constructed levees of the Great Miami River indicates Edward Deeds' faith in his Miami Conservancy District's infrastructure following the devastating flood of 1913.

Open Daily

Monday–Saturday 9:30 am–5:00 pm and Sunday 12:00 pm–5:00 pm

Closed January 1, Thanksgiving Day, December 24, 25, and 31

1000 Carillon Blvd., Dayton, OH 45409

www.daytonhistory.org   937.293.2841

Below: Constantly growing, four historic structures were transported from the Kettering-Moraine Museum to Carillon Park in 2009. The move was a literal parade of homes.